George Petrie

**Church And State in Early Maryland**

George Petrie

**Church And State in Early Maryland**

ISBN/EAN: 9783337004392

Printed in Europe, USA, Canada, Australia, Japan

Cover: Foto ©ninafisch / pixelio.de

More available books at **www.hansebooks.com**

# CHURCH AND STATE

IN

# EARLY MARYLAND

# JOHNS HOPKINS UNIVERSITY STUDIES

IN

## HISTORICAL AND POLITICAL SCIENCE

**HERBERT B. ADAMS, Editor**

---

History is past Politics and Politics present History.—*Freeman*

---

## TENTH SERIES

### IV

# CHURCH AND STATE

IN

# EARLY MARYLAND.

By GEORGE PETRIE, Ph. D.

*Professor of History, Alabama Polytechnic Institute.*

BALTIMORE

THE JOHNS HOPKINS PRESS

PUBLISHED MONTHLY

April, 1892

*50140*

THE FRIEDENWALD CO., PRINTERS,

BALTIMORE.

# CHURCH AND STATE IN EARLY MARYLAND.

The purpose of this monograph is to trace the relation of
State to Church in Maryland from the foundation of the
colony in 1634 down to the establishment of the Church of
England in 1692. The subject will be treated under the
following heads:

1. The Provisions of the Charter with regard to Religion.

2. The Period from the Founding of the Colony to the
Act of Toleration in 1649. Here the object will be to trace
the development of religious freedom.

3. The Period from the Act of Toleration in 1649 to the
Protestant Revolution of 1689. During this period the
object will be to trace the history of the religious toleration
already established.

4. The Protestant Revolution and the Establishment of the
Church of England in 1692.

The subject will be examined under these four heads in
the order in which they are given above. At the end of
each will be stated our conclusions on that division. A brief
summary at the close of the paper will give the conclusions
that we believe may be drawn from the whole inquiry.

### I.—THE PROVISIONS OF THE CHARTER WITH REGARD TO RELIGION.

The following extracts give the parts that bear directly on
the question:

(a) "*Whereas* our well beloved and right trusty subject
*Cecelius Calvert*, Baron of *Baltimore*, in our kingdom of Ire-

land, son and heir of *George Calvert*, knight, late Baron of
*Baltimore*, in our said kingdom of Ireland, treading in the
steps of his father, being animated with a laudable and pious
zeal for extending the Christian religion, and also the terri-
tories of our empire, hath humbly besought leave of us, that
he may transport, by his own industry and expense, a numerous colony of the English nation, to a certain region, herein-
after described, in a country hitherto uncultivated, in the
parts of America, and partly occupied by savages, having no
knowledge of the Divine Being, and that all that region, with
some certain privileges and jurisdictions appertaining unto
the wholesome government and state of his colony and region
aforesaid, may by our royal highness be given, granted, and
confirmed unto him, and his heirs.   *Know ye*, therefore," etc.[1]

(*b*) "Also, we do *grant*, and likewise *confirm* unto the said
Baron of *Baltimore*, his heirs and assigns, all islands and
islets, &c.   And furthermore, the *Patronages* and *Advowsons*
of all churches which (with the increasing worship and religion
of *Christ*), within the said region, islands, islets and limits
aforesaid, hereafter shall happen to be built; together with
license and faculty of erecting and founding churches, chapels,
and places of worship, in convenient and suitable places,
within the premises, and of causing the same to be dedicated
and consecrated according to the ecclesiastical laws of our
kingdom of *England*."

(*c*) "And if, peradventure, hereafter it may happen that
any doubts 'or questions should arise concerning the true
sense and meaning of any word, clause, or sentence contained
in this our present *charter*, we will charge and command
*That* interpretation to be applied always, and in all things,
and in all our courts and judicatories whatsoever, to obtain
which shall be judged to be the more beneficial, profitable,
and favorable to the aforesaid now Baron of *Baltimore*, his
heirs and assigns; provided always, that no interpretation

---

[1] These extracts are taken from the translation of the charter given in
Scharf, I., p. 53 *seq.*

thereof be made, whereby *God's* holy and true Christian religion, or the allegiance due to us our heirs and successors, may in any wise suffer by change, prejudice or diminution."

The *first* extract is plainly nothing more than a formal introduction, such as frequently occurs in the charters of the time. As to the precise meaning of the *second* extract there has been a wide difference of opinion. The grant of the " license and faculty " of erecting and consecrating churches " according to the ecclesiastical laws of our kingdom of England " may imply :

1. That churches *must* be thus and only thus erected and consecrated.

2. That *if* churches be erected and consecrated it *must* be according to the ecclesiastical laws of England.

3. That *if* churches be erected and consecrated it *may* be according to the ecclesiastical laws of England.

The first interpretation would practically establish the Church of England. The second would almost necessarily prevent the establishment of any other church. The third would grant permission for the establishment of the Church of England, but would not exclude other churches from being established.

The point of the *third* extract is in its last clause—" provided always, that no interpretation thereof be made, whereby *God's* holy and true Christian religion, or the allegiance due to us, our heirs and successors, may in any wise suffer by change, prejudice or diminution."

What is meant by " God's holy and true Christian religion " (" Sacro sancta dei et vera Christiana religio ") ? Does this include all decent forms of Christianity ? Or is the king, being head of the Church of England, supposed to consider *it* as the " holy and true Christian religion," and does he by this phrase in the charter refer only to the Church of England ? Some light may be thrown on these extracts by other charters of the time.

With the *second* extract it is interesting to compare the

charter of Avalon,[1] granted to Baltimore, April 7, 1623, and the grant of New Albion,[2] given to Plowden, June 21, 1634. All these are very much alike, and each was probably modeled on its predecessor. All three contain the clause granting "the *Patronages* and *Advowsons* of all churches which (with the increasing worship and religion of *Christ*), within the said regions, islands, islets and limits aforesaid, hereafter shall happen to be built." But only the Maryland charter has the rest of the clause concerning the dedication according to the ecclesiastical laws of England. In 1624 Baltimore joined the Roman Catholic Church. Now, since the charter of Avalon, granted him before that event, omits the dedication clause, the Maryland charter granted him when he was a Catholic inserts it, and two years later Plowden's charter, closely resembling it in other respects, omits this clause; it therefore seems probable that the clause was inserted as a precaution of some sort against Roman Catholicism, but its effectiveness in this sense would vanish unless it excluded dedication and consecration other than by the laws of England. Therefore we may eliminate, as *probably* not intended, the third of the interpretations given above. And as the first interpretation seems scarcely a legitimate construction of the phraseology, the second is left as the probable meaning of the clause, namely, that if churches be erected and consecrated, it *must* be according to the ecclesiastical laws of England.

With the *third extract* we may compare:

1. A clause in the letters patent granted by Queen Elizabeth to Sir Walter Raleigh in 1584: "So always as said statutes, laws, and ordinances may be, as neere as conveniently may be, agreeable to the laws, statutes, government, or pollicie of England, and also, so as they be not against the Christian faith, nowe professed in the Church of

---

[1] Given in Scharf, I., 35. (Copies in Latin and English are in the Calvert Papers.)

[2] Given in the Latin in Penn. Mag. of Hist. and Biog., Vol. VII., 55.

England, nor in any wise to withdraw any of the people of those lands from the allegiance of us, our heirs," etc.[1]

2. A clause in the Instructions for the Government of the Colonies, given in 1606 : "and wee doe specially ordaine, charge, and require, the said president and councells, and the ministers of the said several colonies respectively, within their several limits and precincts, that they, with all diligence, care and respect, doe provide, that the true word and service of God and Christian faith be preached, planted, and used, not only within every of the said several colonies, and plantations, but alsoe as much as they may amongst the salvage people which doe or shall adjoine unto them, or border upon them, according to the doctrine, rights, and religion now professed and established within our realme of England," etc.[2]

3. A part of the Virginia charter of 1609 : "And lastly because the principal effect which we can desire or expect of this action, is the conversion and reduction of the people in those parts unto the true worship of God and Christian religion in which respect we should be loath, that any person should be permitted to pass, that we suspected to effect the superstitions of Rome : we do hereby declare," etc.[3]

4. A clause in the grant of Maine to Gorges, April 3, 1639 : " No interpretation being made of any word or sentence whereby God's holy and true Christian religion now taught, professed and maintained the fundamental lawes of this realm or our allegiance to us our heirs and successors may suffer prejudice or diminucon."[4]

---

[1] Given in Streeter : Maryland 200 Years Ago.  Appendix.

[2] Given in Brown : The Genesis of the United States.  Vol. I., 67–8.

[3] Given in Lucas : Charters of the Old English Colonies in America, p. 18.

[4] This is taken from Hazard, Vol. I., 455.  He has it " whereby God's word, true Christian religion," etc. ; but as in his version of Plowden's charter for New Albion he translates the Latin "sacro sancta dei et vera Christiana religio " by " the word of God and true Christian religion," I have concluded that he is here translating the same Latin, and have given it the usual rendering.

These passages make it clear that, however the charter might be interpreted on its face, if taken in the light of similar documents of the time, "God's true and holy Christian religion" means the Church of England.

But apart from these passages which bear directly on the relation of State to Church, there are two others that bear on it indirectly:

1. After giving the Proprietary the right to make laws with the assent of the freemen of the Province, it continues:

"So, nevertheless, that the laws aforesaid be consonant to reason, and be not repugnant or contrary, but (so far as may be) agreeable to the laws, statutes, customs and rights of this our kingdom of England."

2. Further on occurs the following passage:

"We will also, out of our more abundant grace, for *us*, our heirs and successors, do firmly charge, constitute, ordain and command, that the said *Province* be of our allegiance; and that all and singular the subjects and liege-men of *us*, our heirs and successors, transplanted or hereafter to be transplanted into the *Province* aforesaid, and the children of them, and of others their descendants, whether already born there or hereafter to be born, be and shall be natives and liege-men of *us* our heirs and successors, of our kingdom of England and Ireland; and in all things shall be held treated, reputed and esteemed as the faithful liege-men of *us*, and our heirs and successors, born within our kingdom of England; also lands, tenements, revenues, services, and other hereditaments whatsoever, within our kingdom of England, and other our dominions, to inherit, or otherwise purchase, receive, take, have, hold, buy and possess, and the same to use and enjoy, and the same to give, sell, alien, and bequeath: and likewise all privileges, franchises and liberties of this our kingdom of England, freely, quietly, and peaceably to have and possess, and the same may use and enjoy in the same manner as our liege-men born, or to be born within our said kingdom of England, without impediment, molestation, vexation, impeachment, or grievance of *us*, or any of our heirs or successors; any statute, act, ordinance, or provision to the contrary thereof notwithstanding."

The first of these is so vague as to be satisfied by almost any arrangement with regard to church. But the second gives the inhabitants of the province the right to all the privileges of native-born Englishmen, and it is difficult to see how this can be so construed as to exclude the right to the establishment of the Church of England.

To sum up : the charter *probably* requires that if churches be erected and consecrated, it must be according to the ecclesiastical laws of England; it directs that no interpretation be put upon it whereby the Church of England may suffer by change, prejudice, or diminution ; and it gives the inhabitants of the province the same right as native-born Englishmen to whatever privileges accompany an establishment.

But in the uncertain state of political and religious affairs in England at that time it would have been a difficult matter to say just what were the rights of the Church of England that must not be infringed upon, and just what privileges all Englishmen could claim from an establishment. Moreover, it was not a time when things turned on technical interpretation of written documents. Historical forces were at work, and these, in connection with the policy of the administration and the temper of the colonists, were, after all, to determine the relation of Church and State in Maryland. It is our task, then, to trace the development of this relation, and this brings us to our second division.

## II.—THE PERIOD FROM THE FOUNDING OF THE COLONY TO THE ACT OF TOLERATION IN 1649.

This is the period of the development of religious toleration.

1. Lord Baltimore's intention with regard to religious freedom is clearly shown by a letter of his son Charles, written in 1678. It says: "My father, albeit he had an

absolute liberty given to him and his heirs to carry thither any persons out of any the dominions that belonged to the Crown of England who should be willing to go thither, yet when he came to make use of this liberty he found very few who were inclined to go and seat themselves in those parts but such as for some reason or other, could not live with ease in other places and of these a great part were such as could not conform in all particulars to the several laws of England relating to religion. Many there were of this sort of people who declared their willingness to go and plant themselves in this province so as they might have a general toleration settled there by a law by which all of all sorts who professed Christianity in general might be at liberty to worship God in such manner as was most agreeable with their respective judgments and consciences, without being subject to any penalties whatever - for their so doing, provided the civil peace were preserved. And that for the securing the civil peace, and preventing all heats and feuds which were generally observed to happen amongst such as differ in opinions upon occasion of reproachful nicknames, and reflecting upon each other's opinions, it might by the same law be made penal to give any offense in that kind. These were the conditions proposed by such as were willing to go and be the first planters of this province; and without the complying with these conditions, in all probability this province had never been planted. To these conditions my father agreed; and accordingly soon after the first planting of this province these conditions, by the unanimous consent of all who were concerned, were passed into a law; and the inhabitants of this province have found such effects from this law, and from the strict observance of it, as well in relation to their quiet as in relation to the farther peopling of this province, that they look on it as that whereon alone depends the preservation of their peace, their properties, and their liberties.'"[1]

---

[1] See Archives of Maryland: Council II., 267–8. In this quotation the spelling and punctuation have been modernized.

In the light of this should be taken the following extracts from a letter written in 1638 by Cornwalleys, one of the most prominent of the original settlers: " Perhaps this fault hath beene permitted in vs as A favoure toe yr Lo$^p$ whereby you may declare the Sincerety of yr: first pyouse pretence for the Planting of this desert Province, w$^{ch}$ will bee toe much doubted of if you should take Advantage of oure Ignorant and vncontionable proceedeings toe Assume more than wee can Justly giue you.''[1]

And a little further on : " Y$^r$ Lo$^p$ knowes my Securety of Contiens was the first Condition that I expected from this Government.''

In keeping with this are his instructions to the first colonists, from which is taken this extract: " Inpri: His Lo$^{pp}$ requires his said Gouernor & Commissioners th$^t$ in their voyage to Mary Land they be very carefull to preserue vnity & peace amongst all the passengers on Shipp-board, and that they suffer no scandall nor offence to be giuen to any of the Protestants, whereby any iust complaint may heerafter be made, by them, in Virginea or in England, and that for that end, they cause all Acts of Romane Catholique Religion to be done as priuately as may be, and that they instruct all the Romane Catholiques to be silent vpon all accasions of discourse concerning matters of Religion; and that the said Gouernor & Comissioners treate the Protestants w$^{th}$ as much mildness and fauor as Justice will permitt. and this to be obserued at Land as well as at Sea.'' (Calvert Papers, Vol. I., p. 132.)

And in keeping with this liberal policy he offered the same toleration a few years later to such persons from Massachusetts as would moue to Maryland. In proof of this the following extract is given from Gov. Winthrop's Journal for 1643 : " The Lord Bartemore being owner of much land near Virginia, being himself a papist, and his brother, Mr. Calvert the governour there a papist also, but the colony

---

[1] Calvert Papers, p. 172.

consisted both of protestants and papists, he wrote a letter to Captain Gibbons of Boston, and sent him a commission, wherein he made tender of land in Maryland to any of ours that would transport themselves thither, with free liberty of religion, and all other privileges which the place afforded, paying such annual rent as should be agreed upon; but our Captain had no mind to further his desire herein, nor had any of our people temptation that way."[1]

Some time before 1649[2] he seemed also to have promised religious toleration to Puritan refugees from Virginia, for the author of 'Leah and Rachel,' a pamphlet published in 1656, says: "Maryland was courted by them [the Puritans] as a refuge, the Lord Proprietor and his Governor solicited to, and several addresses and treaties made for their admittance and entertainment into that province; their conditions were pitied, their propositions were hearkened to and agreed on, which was, that they should have convenient portions of land assigned them, liberty of conscience, and privilege to choose their own officers, and hold courts within themselves. All was granted them," etc.

These extracts prove that, from the first, Baltimore's plan was to maintain religious toleration in Maryland.

2. But not only was religious toleration promised by Baltimore, it was enforced also in various ways by him, and by the government in the colony, as will be evident from the following facts:

(a) A proclamation was made against all disputes that tended to "cherish a faction in religion." Neither the form nor the precise date of this is known, but it was at least as early as 1638; for in that year we have a full account of the trial of William Lewis, who had quarreled rather violently with two servants on religious questions; and in the record

---

[1] Winthrop's History of New England, ed. by Savage, II., 149.

[2] This was before 1649, because the author of 'Leah and Rachel' says that after they came to Maryland the Puritans participated in the Assembly which passed the Act of Toleration.

of the proceedings occurs the following sentence: "The Captain, likewise, found him to have offended against the public peace, and against the proclamation made for the suppressing of all such disputes tending to the cherishing of a faction in religion; and therefore fined him likewise five hundred pounds to the Lord of the Province."[1]

(b) But religious freedom was maintained in a more thorough way than by mere proclamation. In the oath which governor and councillors were required to take on entering their office, there was a clause which required them to maintain religious toleration in the colony. Exactly when this clause was first inserted in the oath is a disputed point. Chalmers says[2] it was taken in this form "between 1637 and 1657"; but what ground he had for this assertion is not known, and his phraseology is ambiguous. It may mean constantly between 1637 and 1657, or it may mean sometimes between those years. I have searched the records carefully, and find the oath with the toleration clause taken after, but never before, 1648. The following is the clause in question in the oaths for governor and councillors in the form in which it was sent out by Baltimore, August 6, 1648:

"I will not by myself nor any person directly or indirectly trouble molest or discountenance any person whatsoever in the said Province professing to believe in Jesus Christ and in particular no Roman Catholick for or in respect of his or her Religion nor in his or her free exercise thereof within the said Province so as they be not unfaithful to his said Lordship or molest or conspire against the Civil Government Established here under him."[3] Thus far the governor's and the councillor's oaths agree, but the governor's oath contains in addition the following: "nor will I make any difference of Persons in Conferring of Offices Rewards or Favours proceeding from the Authority which his said Lordship hath

---

[1] Archives of Maryland, Provincial Court, II., 38.

[2] Chalmers: Annals, p. 235.

[3] Archives of Md., Council I., 210, 214.

conferred upon me as his Lieu.<sup>t</sup> here for in Respect of their s.<sup>d</sup> Religion Respectively but mearly as I shall find them faithful and well deserving of his said Lordship and to the best of my understanding endowed with moral virtues and abilities fitting for such Rewards Offices or favours wherein my prime aim and end from time to time . . . . . . . shall sincerely be the Advancement of his said Lordships service here and the publick unity and Good of the Province without Partiality to any or any other sinister end whatsoever and if any other Officer or Person whatsoever shall during the time of my being his said Lordships Lieutenant here without my consent or Privity molest or disturb any Person within this Provence professing to believe in Jesus Christ meerly for or in Respect of his or her Religion or the free exercise thereof upon notice or Complaint thereof made unto me I will apply my Power and Authority to Relieve and Protect any Person so molested or troubled whereby he may have right done him for any damage which he shall suffer in that kind & to the utmost of my power will Cause all and every such person or persons as shall molest or trouble any other Person or Persons in that manner to be punished."

3. Promises, proclamations and oaths may very well indicate Baltimore's policy with regard to religious freedom; but equally important with the policy is the way in which that policy is carried out in the concrete cases. And it was not long before the test case arose that was to decide whether this policy was practicable and had behind it energy and discretion enough to give it vitality. The test came in the conflict between canon and civil law. Dr. Wm. Hand Browne puts the case as follows:

" In England, testamentary matters, the appointment of administrators, etc., were under the jurisdiction of the ecclesiastical courts. In Maryland, as yet, there were no ecclesiastics but the Jesuits; were they to have control over all orphans' estates? One of the rights most strongly asserted by the Church of Rome was that priests and church property were amenable to ecclesiastical law only; were they to be put on the same footing as laymen—to be liable to summons, arrest, or distraint, to civil or criminal process in the ordinary courts of law?"[1]

Clearly if such things as testamentary matters are to be in the hands of ecclesiastics, and if priests and church property are to be subject only to ecclesiastical law, ecclesiastical courts must be recognized in the colony. But this would be inconsistent with Baltimore's plans for religious freedom and equality.

Further, from the founding of the colony, the Jesuits, though not numerous, had been zealous and energetic, and had made a number of converts, not only among the colonists, but also among the Indians. "In return, the kings and chiefs had given them immense grants of land, which, in addition to those taken up under the conditions of plantation, were held by Thomas Copley, one of their members, to the use of the order. Here was another danger. Were lands in Maryland to be held by any other title than as grants from the Proprietary? Were great estates to grow up, held in mortmain, always increasing, and never reverting to secular hands?"[2] Baltimore saw the danger of these tendencies and firmly resisted them.[3] In this he was earnestly supported by Mr. Lewgar, his secretary, a Protestant recently converted to Catholicism, as is indicated by the following extract from a letter written in 1628 by Mr. Copley, a Roman Catholic, to Baltimore:

"First there is not any care at all taken, to promote the conuersion of the Indians. to provide or to shew any fauor to Ecclesiasticall persons, or to preserue for the church the Immunitye and priueledges, w^ch she enioyeth euery where else; *But rather M^r Lugar seemeth to defend opinions here,*

---

[1] Browne: George and Cecilius Calvert, p. 103.

[2] Browne: George and Cecilius Calvert, p. 104.

[3] On the contest between the Proprietary and the Jesuits, see Johnson: Foundation of Maryland, pp. 55–94.

*that she hath noe* priueledges *iure diuino.* That bulls Canons
and Casuists are little to be regarded in these cases, because
they speake for themselues, as if others oposing them had noe
selfe interest and therfor must know better what belongs to
the church then she hirselfe. That Priueledge are not due to
the church till the common wealths in w^ch the church is grante
them. And therfor while they grante none, *I doubte that
not only M^r. Lugar, but also some others that I feare adhere to
much* to him, conceaue that they may proceed w^th Ecclesiasticall persons and w^th others, and accordingly they seeme to
resolve to bind them to all there lawes, and to exacte of them
as of others."[1]

The course which Lewgar adopted to attain his ends is thus
described in the record of the Society of Jesus: "Therefore
this Secretary having summoned the Parliament in Maryland,
composed, with few exceptions, of heritics and presided over
by himself, in the name of the Lord Baltimore himself, he
attempted to pass the following laws, repugnant to the Catholic faith and ecclesiastical immunities; That no virgin can
inherit unless she marry's before 29 years of age; that no
ecclesiastic shall be summoned in cause, civil or criminal, before any other than a secular judge; that no ecclesiastic shall
enjoy any privilege, except such as he is able to show *ex Scrip-
tura,* nor to gain anything for the Church, except by the gift
of the Prince, nor to accept any site for a church or cemetery,
nor any foundation from a convert Indian King, nor shall
any one depart from the Province even to preach the Gospel
to the infidels by authority of the See Apostolic, without a
license from the laye Magistrate; nor shall any one exercise
jurisdiction within the Province which is not derived from
the Baron, and such like."[2]

These measures seem never to have become laws, as they do
not appear in the records. But about this time testamentary
matters were, by act of the Assembly of the colony, formally

---

[1] Calvert Papers, p. 162–3.
[2] Johnson: Foundation of Maryland, p. 81.

brought under civil jurisdiction ; for in "an Act ordeining certain laws for the government of this Province," passed by that body in March, 1638-9, and approved by the Proprietary, there occurs the following clause : " The Secretary shall prove wills and grant Administrations and use and appoint all power and means necessary or conducing thereunto." [1]

And in 1640, the civil power assumed control likewise of marriages and the Assembly passed the following act in regulation thereof :

### " An Act touching Marriages.

No partie may Solemnize marriage with any woman afore the banes 3 days before published in some Chappell or other place of the County where publique instnts are used to be notified or else afore oath made & caution entred in the County Court that neither partie is apprentice or ward or pre–contracted or within the forbidden degrees of consanguinity or under govermt, of parents or tutors and certificate of such oath & caution taken from the Judge or Register of the Court upon paine of fine & recompense to the partie grieved."

This act was to endure for two years after the end of this Assembly.   Lewgar's attempt had in large part failed.   But in the contest over the laws which he urged, the Jesuits naturally sided in favor of the canon law, and strove so earnestly to maintain what they regarded as their privileges under that system that Baltimore, who was determined to do away with these privileges, thought it best to obtain their withdrawal from the colony and to have secular priests sent out in their stead.

" The said Baron, with others favorable to his opinions, began to turn his attention to the expulsion of the Fathers, and the introducing others in their stead, who would be more pliable to his Secretary.   Therefore he proceeded last year, to petition the Sacred Congregation of the Propagation of the Faith, in the name of the Catholics of Maryland, to grant a

---

[1] Archives of Maryland, Assembly I., 83.

Prefect and priests of the Secular Clergy, faculties for the same mission, making no mention in the meantime, of the labors of the Fathers undertaken in that harvest, nor expressing the motives which induced him to substitute new priests . . . But the Sacred Congregation, being entirely ignorant of these matters, granted the Petition."[1]

In November, 1641, Baltimore issued new " Conditions of Plantation," containing in the last two sections provisions against holding land in mortmain, and accompanied by an oath which was to be administered to those taking up land, and which bound its taker to receive and hold land from no one except the Proprietary. For some unknown reason the last two sections and the oath seem not to have been published.

When these were received in Maryland, the Governor and Lewgar visited the Jesuits and the whole matter of ecclesiastical privileges was discussed anew. The question was referred by the Jesuits to their Provincial in England, and by him to Rome. Finally the Provincial officially declared that the conditions of plantation and the oath contained nothing which the Jesuits might not comply with, and formally gave up all lands held by them and all right to acquire land except from the Proprietary.

Thus ended the contest over the canon law. Causes testamentary and matrimonial were now formally brought under the jurisdiction of the civil courts, and the Jesuits formally renounced the right to acquire land except with the consent of the Proprietary. On June 20, 1648, new conditions of plantation were sent out and published, containing practically the same sections about mortmain and accompanied by virtually the same oath as in 1641.[2]

The more general question of ecclesiastical privileges was not formally settled, but there were no established clergy and no ecclesiastical courts, so no privileges could really be put into practice; and, furthermore, the policy of the admin-

---

[1] Records of the Society of Jesus, in Johnson, p. 82.
[2] Archives of Maryland, Council I., 226-7.

istration had been emphatically announced on this point, had met with no successful opposition and remained in possession of the field.

4. But in developing religious freedom in the colony, Baltimore and his executives did not work alone. From the first the colonists themselves, through the Assembly, took part in the formation of the policy which should regulate religious affairs.

The existing records of the Assembly proceedings begin in January, 1637–8. There seems to have been some kind of Assembly before this, and it is quite possible that it passed some Act of Toleration. In 1758 the Upper and the Lower Houses were discussing the claims of Papists to consideration in Maryland; and the Upper House said: "After the charter was thus granted to Lord Baltimore, who was then a Roman Catholic, his lordship emitted his proclamation to encourage the settlement of his province, promising therein, among other things, liberty of conscience, and an equal exercise of religion to every denomination of Christians who would transport themselves and reside in his province, and that he would procure a law to be passed for that purpose afterwards. The first or second Assembly that met after the colonists arrived here, some time in the year 1638, a perpetual law was passed, in pursuance of his lordship's promise, and, indeed, such a law was easily obtained from those who were the first settlers. This was confirmed in 1649 and again in 1650."[1]

To this may refer also a sentence in the letter, already quoted, of Charles Calvert, written in 1678. Writing about the demands of the first settlers for a promise of toleration before leaving home, he says: "To these conditions my father agreed; and accordingly soon after the first planting of this province these conditions by the unanimous consent of all who were concerned were passed into a law."

But if any such act were passed before 1637, no trace of it

[1] Given in Scharf, I., 154.

has remained.  The earliest extant act touching religion is this, which was passed in 1637–8 : "Holy Church within this province shall have all her rights and liberties."[1]

In June, 1640, occurs the following : "An Act for Church liberties.  Holy Church within this Province shall have and enjoy all her Rights liberties and Franchises wholy and without Blemish."[2]

The early acts of the Assembly are full of phrases from Magna Charta, and the two acts just quoted are clearly imitations of the same document.  What was their precise meaning the framers themselves would probably have been puzzled to tell.  They doubtless had no very clear or consistent ideas as to the relation of State to Church, and did not draw very sharply the line between creed and conduct. In an act of 1642 for the punishment of "lesse capital offences," sacrilege and sorcery are ranked side by side with homicide, burglary, piracy, etc.  But a certain rough idea of fair play in religious matters appears in an incident recorded in the proceedings of the Assembly in 1641–2: " The petition of the Protestants was read complaining against Mr. Thomas Gerard for taking away the Key of the Chappel and carrying away the Books out of the Chappel and such proceedings desired against him for it as to Justice appertaineth.  Mr Gerard being charged to make answer the house upon hearing of the Prosecutors and his defense found that Mr Gerard was guilty of a misdemeanour and that he should bring the Books and Key taken away to the place where he had them and relinquish all title to them or the house and should pay for a fine 500l tobacco towards the maintenance of the first minister as should arrive."[3]

Also, as has been mentioned in another connection, the Assembly made the regulation of testamentary matters in 1638, and of marriages in 1640, subject to civil law.  These

---

[1] Archives of Maryland, Assembly I., 83.
[2] Archives of Maryland, Assembly I., 96.
[3] Archives of Maryland, Assembly I., 119.

acts are disconnected and show a lack of clear ideas on the fundamental questions of the relation of State to Church ; but there is in them a certain rough love of liberty that is not altogether out of keeping with the great act which constituted the legal corner-stone of religious freedom in Maryland, the Act of 1649.

The provisions of this Act are as follows :[1]

" Acts of Assembly of the 21 of Aprill 1649. Confirmed by the Lord Proprietary by an instrument under his hand & seale 26th of August 1650
Phillip Calvert.

Acts and Orders of Assembly assented unto Enacted and made at a Genāll Sessions of the said Assembly held at St Maries on the one and twentieth day of Aprill Anno Dm 1649 as followeth viz:

" An Act concerning Religion fforasmuch as in a well governed and Xtian Comon Wealth matters concerning Religion and the honor of God ought in the first place to be taken into serious consideracōn and endeavoured to bee settled.    Be it therefore ordered and enacted by the Right Ho[ble] Cecilius Lord Baron of Baltimore absolute Lord and Proprietary of this Province with the advice and consent of this Generall Assembly.    That whatsoever pson or psons within this Province and the Islands thereunto belonging shall from henceforth blaspheme God, that is Curse him, or deny our Saviour Jesus Christ to bee the sonne of God, or shall deny the holy Trinity the ffather sonne and holy Ghost, or the Godhead of any of the said Three psons of the Trinity or the Unity of the Godhead, or shall use or utter any reproachfull Speeches, words or language concerning the said Holy Trinity, or any of the said three psons thereof, shalbe punished with death

---

[1] Archives of Maryland, Assembly I., 244 sq.

and confiscatōn or forfeiture of all his or her lands and goods to the Lord Proprietary and his heires.

" And be it also Enacted by the Authority and with the advise and assent aforesaid, That whatsoever pson or psons shall from henceforth use or utter reproachfull words or Speeches concerning the blessed Virgin Mary the Mother of our Saviour or the holy Apostles or Evangelists or any of them shall in such case for the first offence forfeit ". . .

Here follow the various penalties: fines, public whipping, imprisonment, banishment, according to circumstances. "And be it also further enacted by the same authority advise and assent that whatsoever pson or psons shall from henceforth uppon any occasion of Offence or otherwise in a reproachful manner or Way declare call or denominate any pson or psons whatsoever inhabiting residing traffiqueing trading or comerceing within this Province or within any the ports, Harbors, Creeks or Havens to the same belonging an heritick, Scismatick, Idolator, puritan, Independant, Prespiterian popish priest, Jesuite, Jesuited papist, Lutheran, Calvenist, Anabaptist, Brownist, Antinomian, Barrowist, Roundhead, Sepatist or any other name or term in a reproachfull manner relating to matter of Religion shall for every such Offence forfeit ". . .

And then follow the penalties : fine, public whipping, and imprisonment, according to circumstances. "And be it further likewise Enacted by the Authority and consent aforesaid That every person and persons within this Province that shall at any time hereafter pphane the Sabbath or Lords day called Sunday by frequent swearing, drunkennes or by any uncivill or disorderly recreacōn, or by working on that day when absolute necessity doth not require it shall for every such first offence forfeit ". . .

Then follow the penalties : fine, imprisonment and public whipping. Last is the provision for religious toleration :

" And whereas the inforceing of the conscience in matters of Religion hath frequently fallen out to be of dangerous Consequence in those commonwealthes where it hath been practised, And for the more quiett and peaceable government of this Province, and the better to p̄serve mutuall Love and amity amongst the Inhabitants thereof. Be it Therefore also by the Lo: Proprietary with the advise and consent of this Assembly Ordeyned & enacted (except as in this p̄sent Act is before Declared and sett forth) that noe person or psons whatsoever within this Province, or the Islands, Ports, Harbors, Creekes, or havens thereunto belonging professing to believe in Jesus Christ, shall from henceforth bee any waies troubled, Molested or discountenanced for or in respect of his or her religion nor in the free exercise thereof within this Province or the Islands thereunto belonging nor any way compelled to the beliefe or exercise of any other Religion against his or her consent, soe as they be not unfaithfull to the Lord Proprietary, or molest or conspire against the civill Government established or to bee established in this Province under him or his heires.

"And that all and every pson and psons that shall presume Contrary to this Act and the true intent and meaning thereof directly or indirectly either in pson or estate willfully to wrong disturbe trouble or molest any person whatsoever within this Province professing to believe in Jesus Christ for or in respect of his or her religion or the free exercise thereof within this Province other than is provided for in this Act that such pson or psons soe offending, shalbe compelled to pay trebble damages to the party soe wronged or molested, and for every such offence shall also forfeit 20ˢ sterling in money or the value thereof, half thereof for the use of the Lo: Proprietary, and his heires Lords and Proprietaries of this Province, and the other half for the use of the party soe wronged or molested as aforesaid, Or if the ptie soe offending as aforesaid shall refuse or bee unable to recompense the party soe wronged, or to satisfy such ffyne or forfeiture, then such Offender shalbe severely punished by publick whipping & imprisonmᵗ during the pleasure of the Lord Proprietary, or his Leiuetenãt or cheife Governor of this Province for the tyme being without baile or maineprise."

The act closes with provisions for carrying it out. Like most great constitutional documents, this act is not absolute in its provisions. The toleration which it grants is conditioned in several ways. The benefits are confined to those professing to believe in Jesus Christ; the doctrine of the Trinity must not be denied or reviled, on penalty of death; no reproach may be uttered against the Virgin Mary or the Evangelists; the "Sabbath" must be strictly observed, and, of course, no religion is permitted to interfere with the civil government.

But in spite of, or rather perhaps because of, these limitations, the act concerning religion marked a long step forward. It proved practicable and worked well. Through forty years of strain and stress it remained, with one brief intermission, the constitutional basis of religious freedom. This is not the place to discuss its relation to any ordinance of the English Parliament in 1645, 1647, or any other year, nor to speculate upon its close resemblance to portions of the 'Utopia.' At that time the *idea* of toleration was no longer private property. From the days of the new learning it had entered the minds of many noblemen, and the attempt to trace the provisions of this act to any English precedent would be speculation.

Nor is it possible fully to determine Baltimore's share in its drafting. That many of the acts passed at this and the following sessions of the Assembly were at least based on a body of laws sent out by Baltimore in 1648 for the approval of the colonists, is reasonably certain.[1] That in this body of laws there was "provision made for freedom of consciences," Baltimore himself states.[2] But how far the act as passed by the Assembly corresponded with the provision in the laws sent out by Baltimore cannot definitely be determined. Further,

---

[1] Johnson, p. 113–126.
[2] Johnson, p. 125, and Archives of Md., Assembly I., 263.

in the commission accompanying this body of laws, Baltimore says that they were "proposed" to him for the good and quiet settlement of the colony, and he finding them "very fit to be enacted as laws," submitted them to the Assembly.[1]  It would be interesting to know who "proposed" them, whether it was Baltimore's friend, the Provincial, Father More, as has been suggested by one writer,[2] or the Puritan preacher, Rev. Thomas Harrison, as intimated by another,[3] or some other and unknown person.  But to settle this point the evidence is again insufficient.

Of this much, however, we can be certain : first, the act was essentially in harmony with Baltimore's policy and gave it legal power; second, it was the formal sanction and adoption of that policy by the people of the colony.  It was therefore the formal culmination at once of the policy of the Proprietary and of the legislation of the colonists.

5. Much energy has been devoted to the discussion as to whether the toleration thus established in Maryland was the work of Roman Catholicism or of Protestantism.  The discussion has turned mainly on three points : (*a*) The faith of the colonists before 1649 ; (*b*) the faith of the Assembly of 1649 ; (*c*) the motive of Baltimore's policy.  And although from a constitutional standpoint the question is of small importance, yet it has been so much debated that it may be well to say a few words about it here.

(*a*) As to the faith of the colonists before 1649, the testimony is as follows :

The Provincial Father More writes in 1642, "the affair was surrounded with many and great difficulties, for in leading the colony to Maryland, by far the greater part were heretics."[4]

Father White writes in 1641, "three parts of the people in four at least are heretics."[5]

---

[1] Johnson, p. 116.
[2] Johnson, p. 133-4.
[3] Neill: Maryland not a Catholic Colony, p. 10.
[4] Johnson, p. 32.
[5] Johnson, p. 32.

Governor Winthrop, in 1634, writing in his journal the report of the Maryland settlers which was brought by a vessel on its return from Bermuda, says : " and those who came over were, many of them, Papists, and did set up mass openly."[1]

In a passage already mentioned in ' Leah and Rachel,' a pamphlet published in 1656, Mr. Hammond describes the coming to Maryland of Virginia Puritans, and the Assembly of 1649, held after their arrival, and says : " An Assembly was called throughout the whole country after their coming over (consisting as well of themselves as the rest), and because there were some few Papists that first inhabited there themselves, and others being of different judgments, an act passed," etc.

In 1700 it was the testimony of old settlers that " some, though but few, Papists were at the first seating."

Governor Sharpe writes in 1758 : " It might, perhaps, be unknown, if not to the authors, at least to some of the propagators of the above-mentioned report, that the people who first settled in this province were, for the most part, Roman Catholics, and that, though every other sect was tolerated, a majority of the inhabitants continued Papists till the revolution."[2]

Chalmers says in the ' Annals ': " The first emigration, consisting of about two hundred gentlemen of considerable fortune and rank, with their adherents, who were composed chiefly of Roman Catholics, sailed from England, in November, 1632."[3]

From this apparently conflicting testimony we turn to circumstantial evidence. Here no conclusion can be drawn *a priori* as to who would take advantage of the refuge offered in Maryland, for others besides Roman Catholics failed to find in England the religious freedom they desired. Nor can

---

[1] Winthrop, I., 134.
[2] Sharpe Correspondence, II., 315 (in Archives of Maryland).
[3] Chalmers: Annals, p. 207.

any just inference be drawn from the oath administered by the 'London Searcher' to 128 of the first settlers as they were about to sail from England, for that oath was merely the oath of *allegiance*, as the 'Searcher' himself states in his official report.[1]  This might readily have been taken by any Catholic, and was distinct from the oath of Supremacy, which no true Catholic could take, as may be seen from the Massachusetts charter of 1628, which grants power to certain officials "to administer and give the oath and oaths of supremacie and allegiance or either of them, to all and every person and persons," etc.[2]

To infer a Protestant majority from the case of Ingle's rebellion is on many accounts absurd.  It is also impossible to infer the religion of the colonists before 1649 from the proportion after that date, because after 1650 there occurred large accessions of Protestants.

A few facts, however, are reasonably certain.  On the one hand, Kent Island was originally settled by Protestants, and a considerable number of Puritans came from Virginia before 1649.  On the other hand, most of the prominent men during the early years of the colony were Catholics, and the zeal of the Jesuits made many converts.  Father White says in 1638: "Of the Protestants who came from England this year, almost all have been converted to the faith."[3]

To sum up, the evidence is not of such a character as to warrant a positive decision as to the relative numbers of Protestants and Catholics in the colony before 1649, but after balancing the testimony and considering the indirect evidence it seems probable that numerically the Protestants were in the majority, but the influence and power of the Catholic minority were greater than their numerical proportion would indicate.

(*b*) As to the faith of the members of the Assembly of 1649

---

[1] Scharf, I., 67.

[2] Lucas: Charters, etc., p. 42.

[3] Given in Neill: Maryland not a Catholic Colony, p. 3.

which passed the Act of Toleration, it is reasonably certain that the Roman Catholics were somewhat in the majority. But here again the precise proportion is uncertain.[1]

(c) Touching the motive which lay behind Baltimore's policy of toleration, little need be said. No one can doubt the sincerity of his faith, for he remained a Catholic when it was notably against his interests to do so. That he was a statesman and diplomat of much resource and ability is proved by the success with which he directed his course during the stormiest and most intricate period of English history. To his interest in the temporal welfare of the colony the inhabitants themselves testified on several occasions. But neither sectarian zeal nor mercenary motives seem sufficient to account for his course. His firm stand in favor of toleration, maintained with consistency and impartiality for forty years against Jesuit and Puritan alike, seems to indicate something more and better than a wily policy which uses the cloak of toleration to protect a single creed. In a word, the only probable explanation of his policy seems to be found in that policy. It was toleration chiefly for the sake of toleration.

In closing this second main division of the subject, the conclusions reached may be summarized as follows: From the beginning Baltimore intended that the colonists should enjoy religious freedom. This policy he maintained by proclamation and oaths, and successfully enforced against the claims of canon law. His policy was gradually sanctioned by the legislation of the colonists, and both his policy and their legislation culminated in the Act of 1649, which was a measure not of absolute but of large toleration.

---

[1] See the investigations of Mr. Davis in his 'Day Star.'

### III.—THE PERIOD FROM THE ACT OF 1649 TO THE
### PROTESTANT REVOLUTION OF 1689.

In treating this period the object will be to trace the changes that took place in the policy of toleration already established and to examine its practical working. The chief points of interest will be the fate of this religious freedom under Puritan control from 1654 to 1656, the status of Jews and Quakers, and the effort made about 1676 to establish the Church of England.

#### 1. *Religious Freedom under Puritan Government* (1654–6).

It is needless to trace here in detail the events that placed the government of Maryland in Puritan hands. No attempt will be made to determine the right or the wrong of what has, perhaps rightly, been called the Puritan Rebellion. With political events as such this paper is not concerned. For our purpose it is sufficient to notice that this revolution in the government was caused, not by religious oppression, which under the circumstances would have been absurdly impolitic, and is sufficiently disproved by the previous policy of the government and by the statement of a number of Protestants in the Protestant Declaration of 1650,[1] but by the following three things :

1. The intolerant spirit of the growing Puritan element in the colony, "while joyfully accepting freedom of worship for themselves, they overlooked the fact that their neighbors, of a different way of thinking, had freedom of worship also."[1] They had " scruples of conscience " about a variety of things. " The fact, also, that the government which they had agreed to support was bound not to molest Roman Catholics, caused them many searchings of heart lest they should be incurring the guilt of permission."[2]

2. The contemporary events of the Puritan Revolution in

---

[1] Given in Scharf, I., 181.

[2] Browne : George and Cecilius Calvert, p. 139.

England, which at once fired their discontented and intolerant spirits, and by impeding the Proprietary's movements, gave them their opportunity.

3. The use which was made of these two elements of discord by Claiborne and other enemies of the government.

These facts are so generally admitted by the best historians that it is unnecessary to cite the evidence in proof of them.

Turning to what most concerns our purpose, the *legislation* under the Puritan government, we find that the Assembly met in October, 1654; that from it were excluded all such "as have borne Armes in Warr against the Parliament or doe profess the Roman Catholic Religion ";[1] that it repealed the Act of 1649[2] and substituted the following *Act concerning Religion* :[3]

" It is Enacted and Declared in the Name of his Highness the Lord Protector with the Consent and by the Authority of the present Generall Assembly that none who profess and Exercise the Popish Religion Commonly known by the Name of the Roman Catholick Religion can be protected in this Province by the Lawes of England formerly Established and yet unrepealed nor by the Government of the Commonwealth of England Scotland and Ireland and the Dominions thereunto belonging Published by his Highness the Lord protector but are to be restrained from the Exercise thereof, Therefore, all and Every person or persons Concerned in the Law aforesaid are required to take notice.

" Such as profess faith in God by Jesus Christ (though Differing in Judgment from the Doctrine worship & Discipline publickly held forth shall not be restrained from but shall be protected in the profession of the faith) & Exercise of their Religion so as they abuse not this Liberty to the injury of others. The Disturbance of the publique peace on their part, Provided that this Liberty be not Extended to

---

[1] Archives, Council I., 313.

[2] Archives, Assembly I., 351.

[3] Archives, Assembly I., 340–1.

popery or prelacy nor to such as under the profession of Christ hold forth and practice Licentiousness."

Comparing this with the Act of 1649, the most striking difference is that, whereas the earlier act gave religious freedom to all professing to believe in Jesus Christ, this one expressly prohibits the exercise of the Roman Catholic religion. On the other hand, this act altogether omits the extreme provisions of the other with regard to blasphemy and reproaches uttered against the Virgin or the Evangelists, as also those touching recriminations and the observance of the Sabbath. Swearing is treated, according to the early custom of the colony, as disorderly conduct and is provided against in a separate and moderate act.[1] The observance of the "Sabbath" is also provided for in a separate act as strict as the provisions of the act of 1649 : "Noe work shall be done on the Sabbath day but that which is of Necessity and Charity to be done no Inordinate Recreations as fowling, fishing, hunting or other, no shouting of Gunns be used on that day Except in Case of Necessity."[2]

On the whole, the act of 1654 is the same as that of 1649 with two exceptions :

1. It omits the harsh provisions against blasphemy.

2. It excludes Catholics from its protection.

Both acts provide that religious liberty shall not infringe upon the rights of the civil government.

After a series of events which concern only the political history of the colony, Baltimore, on November 30, 1657, regained possession of the government, and the former régime was restored. Foreseeing his restoration, he had on October 23, 1656, ordered the act of 1649 to be again observed;[3] and in the articles of settlement of November 30, 1657, occurs the provision (of which the revolutionists were now glad

---

[1] Archives, Assembly I., 343.

[2] Archives, Assembly I., 343.

[3] Archives of Md., Council I., 325.

cnough to avail themselves) that he should never consent to its repeal.[1]

Thus the period of Puritan control passed away without leaving any *formal* change in the relation of State to Church. But in less tangible ways its effects survived. No repeal of laws can do away with the bitter feelings that arise in a civil war, especially if the parties be separated by religious as well as political differences. And the result of the strife that attended this revolution is to be found in a feeling of intolerance and dissatisfaction, which may be traced with more or less clearness down to the Revolution of 1689.

## 2. *The Status of Jews and Quakers.*

The religious liberty granted by the act of 1649 was, as has been said, not absolute. It was limited by two chief conditions : profession of the Christian religion and submission to the civil government. Nor were these limitations unimportant. The first excluded the Jew, and the second bore heavily upon the Quaker. To examine the status of these two classes is to trace, then, in part the practical operation of the act.

There seem to have been very few Jews in Maryland during this period, and the case of Dr. Lumbrozo will be sufficient to show their condition. Mr. Davis, in a note in his ' Day Star,' thus states the case : " In the text I have referred to Dr. Lumbrozo, the well known Jew (for he seems to have observed no secrecy), who lived some time in Maryland, without rebuke from the government, in the usual exercise of his calling, and of the right to institute actions in the civil court. We cannot doubt he was also allowed the *quiet* enjoyment of his religion. But he was accused of blasphemy, and although he fortunately escaped a trial, in consequence of the pardon accompanying the proclamation in favor of Richard, the son of the Lord Protector—a proclamation which

---

[1] Archives of Md., Council I., 334.

was issued but a few days after the accusation—the case is one which was instituted under the act of 1649." [1]

The case of the Quakers is not so readily disposed of. Their large numbers and the changes which their status underwent warrant a fuller treatment. We shall therefore state the early policy of the government towards them, then say a few words as to its significance, and finally trace its later development. The Quakers first entered Maryland about 1657.[2] In that year some missionaries came from Virginia and rapidly made proselytes. Thus arose a sect whose religious scruples brought them into conflict with the civil government on two points : taking oaths and bearing arms. Both these things were vitally connected with the system on which the government was administered, and the law was accordingly enforced against them.[3] In the first year (1658), according to Besse, some forty persons at least were punished, chiefly by fines, but sometimes by whipping.

As to the significance of these facts several things are to be said.

1. The rise of the Quakers was so sudden and their tenets so novel that they were not fully understood. They seemed merely insolent fellows who "at the Court, in contempt of an order then made and proclaimed, would presumptuously stand covered," and asserted that "they were governed by God's lawe and the light within them and not by man's lawe." [4]

2. Their claims to exemption from military duty and from the customary oaths struck squarely at what were considered two essential features of the colonial government.

3. To allow the customary oaths to be omitted by jurymen or in testamentary matters would have been a dangerous innovation on English Common Law, and might on that

---

[1] Day Star, p. 65.

[2] See J. S. Norris, The Early Friends in Maryland.

[3] See Archives of Md., Council I., 348–50, 352, 362, and the cases cited in Besse, Sufferings of the Quakers, II., 278–80.

[4] Archives, Council I., 352.

ground have been construed as contrary to the charter and
have involved the Proprietary in complications in England.

4. As the Upper House said in 1662,[1] the omission of oaths
would have rendered "all Testimonyes taken in this Province
invalid in any court in England or other plantations."

But what could, or ought to, have been done it is not our
duty to decide. The policy that was adopted by the government has been stated. The changes that took place in this
policy must now be traced. The Quakers increased rapidly
in numbers and influence. Fox's visit to Maryland in 1672
greatly strengthened them.[2] Prominent men became Quakers
and Quakers became prominent men.[3] As they increased
in influence and were better understood, the attitude of the
government toward them became more favorable. Their chief
trouble seems to have arisen from the necessity of taking
oaths. Several attempts were made to substitute "Yea" and
"Nay"; for example, in 1662,[4] in 1674,[5] and in 1681.[6] These
all failed, and those who refused the oaths were fined.[7]

In 1688 Baltimore issued a proclamation dispensing with
oaths in testamentary cases.[8] This gave some relief and was
gratefully acknowledged by the Quakers.[9] But although the
fact that Thurston was excused from the oath of fidelity in
1688 [10] indicates an occasional leniency of administration, yet
not until 1702 was an act passed entirely relieving them from
all necessity of taking oaths.

---

[1] Archives, Assembly I., 437.

[2] Fox, Journal, II., 124.

[3] Day Star, 77, and Norris, p. 15.

[4] Archives of Maryland, Assembly I., 436-7.

[5] Archives of Maryland, Assembly II., 355-6, 424, 426, 428, 431-2, and
Norris, p. 19 and note.

[6] Archives of Maryland, Assembly III., 174, 175, 179, 184-5, and Besse,
II., 387.

[7] Besse, II., 387.

[8] Archives, Council III., 57.

[9] Besse, II., 387.

[10] Council III., 63.

### 3. *The Attempt to Establish the Church of England* (1676).

In examining this movement we shall consider, first, its history; second, its results; and third, the state of religious freedom in the colony at the time.

1. The movement made in 1676 to introduce an established church seems not to have been the first of its kind in the history of Maryland.

In the Colonial Assembly of 1661 there had been introduced an "Act for Mayntenance for Ministers," which was voted to be "altogether insufficient and short of the thing aymed att."[1]

In 1666 a motion had been made "Concerning the settling of ministers in every County of this Province," as is indicated by the following entry in the records:

"A Member of the howse informes the Speaker that Mr Bretton Clerk of the Assembly did reuyle Mr Rob$^t$ Burle, calling him ffactious fellow. Vppon a Motion wch the sd Burle made in this howse, Concerning the settling of Ministers in Every County of this Province. The wch was attested by Mr Willm Coursey, one of the Members of this howse.

"Uppon wch Informaōn the howse tooke itt into their Consideraōn, And vppon Mr. Brettons humble submission to the howse, & tht perticular Member, & his humble request that this howse would please att this time to remitt the sd offense. The wch hee hereby acknowledges hee is guilty of. And that hee did not speake or utter those words out of any abusive intent, But [occa]sioned through some distemper att that [time]."[2]

Both these motions seem to have failed, and are important only as forerunners of the events which cluster about the year 1676. To these we now pass. On May 25, 1676, the Rev. Mr. Yeo, a clergyman of the Church of England, who resided in Maryland, wrote the following letter to the Archbishop of Canterbury:

---

[1] Archives, Assembly I., 404–6.
[2] Archives, Assembly II., 86.

" Most Reverend Father

" Pleased to Pardon this Presumption of mine in presenting to Yo$^r$ serious view these Rude & indigested lines w$^{ch}$ (with humble Submission) are to acquaint Yo$^r$ Grace with the Deplorable estate & condition of the Province of Maryland for want of an established Ministry here are in this Province tenn or twelve Countys & in them at least twenty thousand Soules & but three Protestant ministers of us th$^t$ are Conformable to the Doctrine & Discipline of the Church of England others there are (I must confess) tht Runn before they are Sent & Pretend they are Ministers of the Gospell th$^t$ never have a Legall call or Ordination to such an holy office, neither (indeed) are they qualified for it being fore the most part such as never understood any thing of learning & yet take upon them to be Dispencers of the word & to Administer Sacrament of Baptisme & sow seeds of Divission amongst the People & noe law Provided for the Suppression of such in this Province soe th$^t$ here is a great Necessitie of able & learned men to confut the gaine sayer espetially having soe many Profest enemies as the Popish Priests & Jesuits are, who are incoraged & Provided for & the Quaker takes care &. provides for those th$^t$ are Speakers in their conventicles, but noe care is taken or Provision made for the building up Christians in the Protestant Religion by means whereof not only many Dayly fall away either to Popery, Quakerism or Phanaticisme but alsoe the lords day is prophaned, Religion despised, & all notorious vices committed soe th$^t$ it is become a Sodom of uncleaness & a Pest house of iniquity, I doubt not but Yo$^r$ Grace will take it into Consideration & do Yo$^r$ utmost for our Eternall welfare, & now is the time th$^t$ Yo$^r$ Grace may be an instrument of a universall reformation amongst us with greatest facillity Cacillius Lord barron Baltimore, & absolut Proprietor of Maryland being dead & Charles lord Barron of Baltimore & our Governour being bound for England this year (as I am informed) to Receive a farther confirmation of th$^t$ Province from his Majestie at w$^{ch}$ time I Doubt but Yo$^r$ Grace may soe prevaile with him as th$^t$ a maintenance for a

Protestant ministry may be established as well in this Province as in Virginia, Barbados & all other his Majesties Plantations in west indies & then there will be incoragement for able men to come amongst us, & th[t] some Person may have power to examine all such Ministers as shall be admitted into any County or perish in w[t] Diocis & by w[t] Bishop they were Ordained, & to Exhibit their lrs of Orders to testify the Same, as yet I think the Generallitie of the people may be brought by Degrees to a uniformitie, Provided we have more ministers th[t] were truly Conformable to our mother the Church & non but such Suffer to preach amongst us, as for my own part (God is my witness) I have done my utmost indeavour in order there unto, & shall (by God's assistance) whiles I have a being here give manifest Proof of my faithfull Obedience to the Canons & Constitutions of our Sacred Mother, Yet one thing cannot be obtained here (viz) Consecration of Churches & Church Yards to the end th[t] Christians might be Decently buried together, whereas now they bury in the several Plantations where they lived, unless Yo[r] Grace thought it Sufficient to give a Dispensation to some Pious minister (together with ther mañer and form) to do the same, & Confident I am th[t] you will not be wanting in any thing th[t] may tend most to God's Glorie & the goods of the Church by w[ch] you will engage thousands of Soules to pray for Yo[r] Graces everlasting happiness, but especially

“ Yo[r] Most Obedient Son
“ Servt
“ John Yeo ” [1]

The Archbishop undertook the task, and in the following letter commissioned the Bishop of London to attend to the matter :

“ From the Archbishop of Canterbury to the Lord London.
Croydon, August 2nd 1676.
My Lord, The inclosed came lately unto me, and from a

---

[1] Archives, Council II., 130-1.

person altogether unknown. The design therein proposed, seem's very honest and is in itself so laudable that I conceive it concern's us by all means to promote it: If your Lordship shall please to remember it, when the Lord Baltamores affaires comes to be considered of at the Council Table, I make no question but there may be a convenient opportunity to obtain some settled revenue for the Ministry of that place as well as the other plantations; when that is once done, it will be no difficult matter for us to supply them with such as are of competent abilities to undertake the employment and withall such as we know to be both regular and conformable. I bid your Lordship heartily farewel and am My Lord your Lordships

"Most affect. Friend and Brother

"Gilb: Cant:"[1]

Some time in 1676 there was addressed to the king a curious and extravagant "Complaint from Heaven with a Hue and Crye and a petition out of Virginia and Maryland," in which, among other requests, is the following: "That Protestant Ministers and free schools and glebe lands may be errected and established in every country, notwithstanding liberty of conscience and maintained by the people."[2]

The Bishop of London seems to have executed the commission of the Archbishop of Canterbury and to have presented Yeo's letter to the Committee for Trade and Plantations, for on the records, just after the letter from the Archbishop, appears the following entry : "Recd from the Lord London 8. August 1676. With a letter from John Yeo Minister in Maryland to the Archbishop of Canterbury. Read the 19th of July 1677."[3]

He was present at the meeting of this Committee on July 19, 1677, which took the affair into consideration. The following extract from the records gives their proceedings:

[1]Archives of Maryland, Council II., 132.

[2]Archives of Maryland, Council II., 149.

[3]Archives of Maryland, Council II., 132.

" There is read a letter directed to the Archbishop of Canterbury from a Minister of Maryland of the 6th of May 1676 which by a letter from his Grace had been transmitted to my Lord B[p] of London complaining of the abuses in the religion and morality of the inhabitants, occasioned by the discouragement of the Protestant Ministry and want of provision for such as are conformable to the Church of England and praying that care bee taken for the establishing and settlement of the Orthodox religion as in other parts of the West Indies. After which the law of Maryland concerning Religion permitting liberty of conscience and a free exercise of service to all persons and sects professing to beleeve in Jesus Christ. Whereupon the Lord Baltemore is called in who offers a paper declaring the present state of the Christian Religion in Maryland and the difficulty to establish any setled maintenance by law for the Ministry of the Church of England there being so few of that perswasion, among soe great numbers of other sectaries.   Which being read their Lordships take notice of the fitness that a setled maintenance bee provided by an Act of the Country for a sufficient number of Orthodox Ministers, to which my Lord Baltimore seemed to consent and then withdrew.

" Their Lordships doe therefore agree to write a letter to my Lord Baltemore taking notice of the scandalous way of living and desiring his Lordship to give orders that either those Laws now in force be put in execution or that if they be not sufficient to restrain it other Laws may bee enacted to that purpose.

" And whereas there is at present noe setled allowance for Orthodox Ministry their Lord[ps] will desire that Inquiry bee made what number of Protestants that conforme to the Church of England there is at present in his Lord[ps] Province and what allowance they would agree to settle in the several Precincts for the encouragement of learned Ministers and that endeavoure bee made to ascertaine by a law of the Country, a sufficient salary for their subsistence.

"That an account be return'd from those parts of the present number of Protestant families and congregations of the Ministers now settled there what allowances they enjoy and how many others are wanting for the supply of the whole Colony. That their Lord$^{ps}$ bee informed of the state of the several religions dissenting from the Church of England in relation to the number of their adherents, teachers, settlement or provision made for their maintenance And in general of the number condition and perswasions of all Planters. Which account the Lord Baltemore is to require from his Deputy Governor and Council and to return it to their Lordships with all possible speed. Mem$^{dm}$ Their Lo$^{ps}$ think fit that when allowances are settled by law in Maryland and other parts according to the abilityes of the inhabitants some meanes bee found out here for the charitable supply of what shall be wanting for the subsistence of the Ministers. As alsoe the several Governors are to find out some farther encouragement for them when they have been there some time either by assigning them lands or otherwise." [1]

The paper in which Baltemore explained the state of religious affairs in the province is as follows : " Whereupon the Lord Baltemore presents a Paper setting forth the Present State of Religion in Maryland. viz : That for the encouragement of all such persons as were desirous and willing to adventure and transport themselves & families into the Province of Maryland a law there made by the advice and consent of the Delegates of the Freemen concerning Religion, wherein a toleration is given to all persons beleeving in Jesus Christ freely to exercise their Religion & that no person of what judgement soever, beleeving as aforesaid should at any time be molested or discountenanced for or in respect of his Religion or in the free exercise thereof and that noe one should be compelled to the beliefe or exercise of any other against his consent. Upon this Act the greatest part of the people and Inhabitants now in Maryland have settled them-

---

[1] Archives of Maryland, Council II., 261-2.

selves & families there & for these many years this toleration & liberty has been known and continued in the Government of that Province.

" That those Persons of the Church of England there who
at any time have encouraged any Ministers to come over unto
that Province have had several sent unto them as at this time
there are residing there foure that the L$^d$ Baltemore knows
of who have Plantations & settled beings of their owne and
those that have not any such beings are maintained by a
voluntary contribution of their own persuasion, as others of
the Presbiterians, Independents, Anabaptists, Quakers &
Romish Church are.

" That in every Country in the Province of Maryland there
are a sufficient number of Churches and Houses called Meeting Houses for the people there and these have been built
and are still kept in good repaire by a free and voluntary
contribution of all such as frequent the said Churches and
Meeting Houses.

" That the Laws of that Province have been ever made by
the advice and consent of the Freemen by their Delegates
assembled as well as by the Proprietor and his Council and
without the consent of all these no Law there has been made.

" The greatest part of the inhabitants of that Province
(three of four at least) doe consist of Præsbiterians, Independents, Anabaptists and Quakers, those of the Church of England as well as those of the Romish being the fewest, so that
it will be a most difficult task to draw such persons to consent unto a Law, which shall compel them to maintain
Ministers of a contrary persuasion to themselves, they having
already an assurance by that Act for Religion that they have
all freedom in point of Religion and Divine Worship and noe
penalties or payments imposed upon them in that particular.
That in Carolina, New Jersey and Roade Island, the inhabitants for the peopling of those places have had and still have
the same toleration that those in Maryland have." [1]

---

[1] Archives of Maryland, Council II., 183–4.

The final action of the Committee is somewhat more fully stated in the following extract from the letter which they wrote to Baltimore : "Wee are likewise informed of another particular from whenever Wee have reason to beleeve, that this disorderly & wicked kind of living of the Inhabitants proceeds in a great measure; w$^{ch}$ is that there is no custom establisht allowance for the Ministers of the Gospell whereby able, Sober & Learned men might be invited to go over to instruct them, & especially in the Protestant Religion according to the Church of England, w$^{ch}$ is the cause that there is a great want of able Ministers there. As Wee know how fit & necessary it is to have that want supplyed, as Wee likewise think it very convenient that it should be done without Imposing any burden upon the Inhabitants other than that they are willing freely to Settle for the Support of their Ministers. In order whereunto Wee desire that your Lo$^p$ will write to the Governour and Councell of Maryland, to send over an acco$^t$ hither w$^{th}$ as much speed as may bee; How many Ministers of the Protestant Religion according to the Church of England are now w$^{th}$in the s$^d$ Plantacōn & what Settlements and allowances they respectively have ; And to the end they may be Supplyed w$^{th}$ Ministers where they are wanted Wee desire yo$^r$ Lo$^p$ to direct the s$^d$ Govern$^r$ & Councell to take an acco$^t$ of all the Protestant Families there & the value of their respective plantacōns, & then considering their Situations in respect of distance one from the other to see how many Congregations they may make up, that so they may be accordingly Supplyed w$^{th}$ Ministers, And this being done Wee desire your Lo$^p$ to give direction to the s$^d$ Govern$^r$ & Councell to enquire what each respective Congregation will be freely willing to Settle for the Maintenance of an able Minister, And when the s$^d$ persons shall have agreed upon such Certain allowances as afores$^d$, that then upon the desire of the s$^d$ persons s$^d$ Govern$^r$ & Councell doe endeavour to have the same Enacted into a Law as is practised in other his Ma$^{tt}$ platacōns. And of this whole matter wee desire to have an account w[th] as much speed as conveniently may be."[1]

In compliance with the requests contained both in this letter and in a sort of circular letter previously sent him,[2] Baltimore replied[3] on March 26, 1678, that there were no parishes in Maryland, that it was impossible to say precisely what were the relative proportions of the religious sects, and that if he should order an investigation it would disturb the peace of the province, which regarded religious freedom as one of its most cherished rights.

2. The formal result of the whole movement is contained in the action of the Committee for Trade and Plantations, who seem, from the extracts above quoted, to have recommended a limited establishment of the Church of England, including only those colonists who were members of that church and supported by them alone. This support was to be assumed voluntarily ; but, once assumed, the government was to see to it that it became incorporated into the law of the colony.

Precisely what force this action had it is difficult to say. Its language is that rather of recommendation than of command, and such Baltimore seems to have considered it, for no steps were taken towards the introduction of any system of establishment.

So far, then, as concerns tangible results, this attempt was a failure. But it was not the first or the last of its kind. It was part of an historical movement, whose growth it shows, and formed a precedent for a later attempt which succeeded.

3. The events and documents of this period furnish some slight but interesting information as to the actual extent of toleration in the colony.

Baltimore's two letters above quoted state that no church is supported by the government, but all depend on voluntary

---

[1]Archives of Maryland, Council II., 253.

[2]Archives of Maryland, II., 129-30.

[3]Archives of Maryland, Council II., 264-9.

contributions (a statement which is confirmed by Yeo's letter), and that the right to religious freedom is jealously guarded by the inhabitants, who consist of Presbyterians, Independents, Anabaptists, Quakers, Members of the Church of England, and Roman Catholics, the last two classes being the smallest in numbers. While taking a firm stand against establishment in any form, Baltimore seems to have welcomed and in other respects to have assisted the clergymen of the Church of England. In 1681 Ambrose Sanderson was recommended [1] to him by the Council as a suitable person to give instruction to the Protestants in the colony. Upon a similar endorsement by the Bishop of London, in 1685 he recommended [2] Paul Bertrand to the government in Maryland. In 1685 he similarly recommended [3] Mr. Willymot.

In connection with these facts should be noted the following assertion of partiality to Roman Catholics : " Letter from the Councill to the Lord Baltimore about partiality to Papists in Maryland.

12th October 1681

After Our hearty Commendacōn to your Lordship, Information having been given unto Us, That there are very few of his Ma$^{tles}$ Protestant Subjects admitted to be of the Councill of the Colony of Maryland, and that there is partiallity and favour shewed on all occasions towards those of the Popish Religion to the discouragement of his Maj$^{tles}$ Protestant Subjects which We hope may proceed from misrepresentacōn yett Wee cannot but take notice thereof unto your Lordship praying and requiring you to cause the same if true to be speedily redressed, and that in the distribution of the Armes and Ammunition (which at the request of your agent Nicholas Lowe Merchant, Wee have permitted to be transported for the Defence of that place) your Lordship do express your trust and confidence in His Maj$^{tles}$ Protestant Subjects by

---

[1] Archives of Maryland, Council II., 300.
[2] Archives of Maryland, Council II., 461.
[3] Archives of Maryland, Council II., 466–7.

putting the said Armes into their hands.    And so being confident of your readiness to answer our expectation in these
particulars Wee bid your Lordship heartily farewell &c.

"Signed," etc.[1]

An investigation revealed the falsity of the charge in
respect to the distribution of offices and arms.    The facts are
still preserved[2] and leave no room for doubt.    The general
charge of discrimination against Protestants is at least rendered improbable by the declaration drawn up by Baltimore[3]
and signed by a number of the prominent colonists who were
members of the Church of England.    This declaration, after
mentioning the charge of partiality, says :

" We, therefore the subscribers professing the Gospell of
Jesus Christ according to the Litturgy of the Church of
England and Protestants against the Doctrine and Practice
of the Church of rome, Subjects also to his Majestie the King
of Great Brittain &c., and residents as aforesaid, esteeming
ourselves (as indeed we are) everyone therein particularly
& nearly concerned, hold ourselves in conscience and duty
obliged by this our impartial, true and sincere remonstrance
or Declaration to unfold the naked truth and to undeceive the
minds of those before whose eyes the mist may have been
against cast, and to purge his Lordship & this Government,
whereof we are, from all those false, scandalous and malicious
aspertions, which the venemous blasts of such inveterate,
malignant, turbulent spirits have cast thereon.    And therefore in the first place, we doe hereby unanimously acknowledge
& publish to the world the general freedom & priviledge
which we and all persons whatsoever Inhabitants of this
Province, of what condicion soever, doe enjoy in our lives,
liberties and estates under this His Lordship's Government
according to the grand priviledges of Magna Charta, as effec-
tually and in as full & ample manner to all intents and

---

[1] Archives of Maryland, Council II., 300-1.
[2] Archives of Maryland, Council II., 309-10.
[3] Archives of Maryland, Assembly III., 314.

purposes, as any of his Majesties Subjects within any part of His Majesties dominions whatsoever with the free & public exercise & enjoyment of our religion whatsoever it be, whether Protestant or other professing the name of Jesus, according to an Act of Assembly of this Province in that case made out & provided, and to which we and the whole Province in general either by ourselves or our representatives in a Generall Assembly have given our assent. We doe also declare and make known that besides our owne experience we have observed his Lordshipp's favours impartially distributed, and Places of Honor, trust and profit conferred on the most qualified for that purpose and service, without any respect or regard had to the religion of the participants, of which generally and for the most part it hath so happened that the Protestants have been the greatest number," etc.[1]

On the whole, it seems probable that these charges originated, as Baltimore claimed,[2] in the really mild measures which had been adopted to put down the rebellion of Fendall and Coode. Our conclusion with regard to this period may be summarized as follows : Puritan control left no permanent constitutional results. Under it the toleration previously established was so restricted as to exclude Roman Catholics. When the government ceased to be exclusively in Puritan hands the old policy was restored. Under it Jews had no religious rights and lived in peace only so long as their belief was overlooked, and Quakers were punished for resisting the civil government by refusing to take oaths and bear arms. The status of the Jew remained practically the same, but that of the Quaker gradually improved until in 1702 he was entirely relieved from all oaths. The attempt to establish the Church of England in 1676 failed, but gave another precedent for the movement which later succeeded. From the Puritan revolution of 1654 to the Protestant revolution of 1689 religious toleration was the policy of the

---

[1] Archives of Maryland, Council II., 353–4.
[2] Archives of Maryland, Council II., 312.

government and seems in the main to have been impartially administered.

## IV.—THE PROTESTANT REVOLUTION OF 1689 AND THE ESTABLISHMENT OF THE CHURCH OF ENGLAND.

To discuss the political history of this revolution is not our task. No attempt will be made to determine how largely it was an echo of contemporary events in England and how largely it was an independent movement arising from local causes. From our standpoint it is interesting for two reasons only : first, because during its course charges were brought of intolerance on the part of the Maryland government; second, because it led to the establishment of the Church of England. But even the first of these two points cannot here be discussed in detail. The records contain many charges of intolerance on the part of Catholics and Protestants, and also many denials ; and to both are attached long lists of attestors' names. But these statements are so colored by passion that no positive conclusion can be drawn from them. Careful investigation of their truth would, in the present incomplete state of the records, necessitate too lengthy a balancing of evidence and would yield too indefinite a result to be attempted here. So far as these charges touch earlier periods, the facts have already been stated. So far as they concern the time of the revolution, they are for that very reason comparatively unimportant, for the administration of a policy during its own death struggle is not of scientific importance.

With regard to the second point mentioned, namely, the establishment of the Church of England, not much *needs* to be said. The revolution put the government exclusively in the hands of the Protestants. At their request the Crown took charge of the province and sent out a royal governor, who upon his arrival summoned an Assembly. The second act[1] passed by this Assembly established the Church of England in

---

[1] See Manuscript Records, Liber L. L. No. I., p. 2 sq.

the province. It was passed June 2, 1692. By it there was " provision made for dividing all the counties into parishes, and the election of vestrymen for each, for the conservation of the church interests; and a poll tax of forty pounds of tobacco imposed upon every taxable of the province, to build churches and sustain their ministers. Thus was introduced, for the first time in Maryland, a church establishment, sustained by law and fed by general taxation." [1]

With this event our task ends. We have examined the relation of Church and State from the founding of the colony to 1692, and have found that religious freedom arose not from the charter but from the policy of the Proprietary, Cecilius Calvert, and from the coöperation of the colonial government and of the colonists themselves; that it culminated in the act of 1649, which granted, not absolute, but large toleration; that this policy was restricted during the period of Puritan control, but was afterwards restored, and, in the main, administered with impartiality; that several attempts were made to introduce an establishment, but they all failed until 1692; that in that year there was introduced by act of Assembly " a church establishment sustained by law and fed by general taxation." To trace the development of that establishment must be a separate undertaking.

---

[1] McMahon's Maryland, I., 243.

# THE JOHNS HOPKINS PRESS,

## BALTIMORE.

I. **American Journal of Mathematics.** S. NEWCOMB, Editor, and T. CRAIG, Associate Editor. Quarterly. 4to. Volume XIV in progress. $5 per annum.

II. **American Chemical Journal.** I. REMSEN, Editor. 8 nos. yearly. 8vo. Volume XIV in progress. $4 per volume.

III. **American Journal of Philology.** B. L. GILDERSLEEVE, Editor. Quarterly. 8vo. Volume XIII in progress. $3 per volume.

IV. **Studies from the Biological Laboratory.** H. N. MARTIN, Editor, and W. K. BROOKS, Associate Editor. 8vo. Volume V in progress. $5 per volume.

V. **Studies in Historical and Political Science.** H. B. ADAMS, Editor. Monthly. 8vo. Vol. X in progress. $3 per volume.

VI. **Johns Hopkins University Circulars.** 4to. Volume XI in progress. $1 per year.

VII. **Johns Hopkins Hospital Bulletin.** 4to. Monthly. $1 per year.

VIII. **Johns Hopkins Hospital Reports.** 4to. $5 per volume.

IX. **Contributions to Assyriology, etc.** Vol. I ready. $8.

X. **Annual Report of the Johns Hopkins University.** Presented by the President to the Board of Trustees.

XI. **Annual Register of the Johns Hopkins University.** Giving the list of officers and students, and stating the regulations, etc. *Published at the close of the academic year.*

---

ROWLAND'S PHOTOGRAPH OF THE NORMAL SOLAR SPECTRUM. New edition now ready. Set of ten plates, mounted. $20.

THE OYSTER. By William K. Brooks. 240 pp. 12mo.; 14 plates. $1.00.

THE TEACHING OF THE APOSTLES (complete facsimile edition). J. Rendel Harris, Editor. 110 pp. and 10 plates. 4to. $5.00, cloth.

OBSERVATIONS ON THE EMBRYOLOGY OF INSECTS AND ARACHNIDS. By Adam T. Bruce. 46 pp. and 7 plates. 4to. $3.00, cloth.

SELECTED MORPHOLOGICAL MONOGRAPHS. W. K. Brooks, Editor. Vol. I. 370 pp. and 51 plates. 4to. $7.50, cloth.

REPRODUCTION IN PHOTOTYPE OF A SYRIAC MS. WITH THE ANTILEGOMENA EPISTLES. I. H. Hall, Editor. $3.00, paper; $4.00, cloth.

STUDIES IN LOGIC. By members of the Johns Hopkins University. C. S. Peirce, Editor. 123 pp. 12mo. $2.00, cloth.

NEW TESTAMENT AUTOGRAPHS. By J. Rendel Harris. 54 pp. 8vo; 4 plates. 50 cents.

THE CONSTITUTION OF JAPAN, with Speeches, etc., illustrating its significance. 48 pp. 16mo. 50 cents.

ESSAYS AND STUDIES. By Basil L. Gildersleeve. 520 pp. small 4to. $3.50, cloth.

---

A full list of publications will be sent on application.

Communications in respect to exchanges and remittances may be sent to The Johns Hopkins Press, Baltimore, Maryland.

### Revue Historique.

*Edited by M. G. Monod, Lecturer at the Ecole Normale Supérieure, Adjunct Director of the Ecole des Hautes Etudes.*

#### 17th Year, 1892.

The "Revue Historique" appears bi-monthly, making at the end of the year three volumes of 500 pages each.

Each number contains: I. Several leading articles, including, if possible, a complete thesis. II. Miscellanies, composed of unpublished documents, short notices on curious historical points. III. Historical reports, furnishing information, as complete as possible, touching the progress of historical studies. IV. An analysis of periodicals of France and foreign countries, from the standpoint of historical studies. V. Critical reports of new historical works.

By original memoirs in each number, signed with the names of authorities in the science, and by reports, accounts, chronicles and analysis of periodicals, this Review furnishes information regarding the historical movement as complete as is to be found in any similar review.

Earlier series are sold separately for 30 frs., single number for 6 frs., numbers of the first year are sold for 9 frs.

Price of subscription, in Postal Union, 33 frs.

### Annales de l'Ecole Libre des Sciences Politiques.

*Published tri-monthly by the coöperation of Professors and Former Pupils of the College.*

#### 7th Year, 1892.

Committee of publication: MM. BOUTMY, Director of the College; LÉON SAY, Member of the Académie Française, formerly Minister of Finance; A. DE FOVILLE, Professor at the Conservatory of Arts and Trades, Chief of the Bureau of Statistics in the Ministry of Finance (Treasury Department); R. STOURM, formerly Inspector of the Finances and Administrator of Indirect Taxes; AUG. ARNAUNÉ; A. RIBOT, Deputy; GABRIEL ALIX; L. RENAULT, Professor at the Law College of Paris; ANDRÉ LEBON, Chief of the Cabinet of the President of the Senate; ALBERT SOREL; PIGEONNEAU, Substitute Professor at the College of Paris; A. VANDAL, Auditor of the First Class.

The subjects treated include the whole field covered by the programme of instruction: Political Economy, Finance, Statistics, Constitutional History, Public and Private International Law, Law of Administration, Comparative Civil and Commercial Legislation, Legislative and Parliamentary History, Diplomatic History, Economic Geography, Ethnography. The Annals besides contain Bibliographical Notices and Foreign Correspondence.

Subscription in Postal Union, 19 frs.

### Revue Philosophique de la France et de l'Etranger.

*Edited by TH. RIBOT, Professor at the College of France.*

#### 17th Year, 1892.

The "Revue Philosophique" appears monthly, and makes at the end of each year two volumes of about 680 pages each.

Each number of the "Revue" contains: 1. Essays. 2. Accounts of new philosophical publications, French and foreign. 3. Complete accounts of periodicals of foreign countries as far as they concern philosophy. 4. Notes, documents, observations. The earlier series are sold separately at 30 frs., and at 3 frs. by number. In Postal Union, 33 frs. Subscriptions to be paid in advance.

Payment may be for the periodicals through postal orders. The publisher will allow all expenses for money orders to be charged to him.

# THE AMERICAN JOURNAL OF ARCHÆOLOGY

AND OF THE

## HISTORY OF THE FINE ARTS.

---

The Journal is the organ of the Archæological Institute of America and of the American School of Classical Studies at Athens, and it will aim to further the interests for which the Institute and the School were founded. It treats of all branches of Archæology and Art History: Oriental, Classical, Early Christian, Mediæval and American. It is intended to supply a record of the important work done in the field of Archæology, under the following categories: I. Original Articles; II. Correspondence from European Archæologists; III. Reviews of Books; IV. Archæological News, presenting a careful and ample record of discoveries and investigations in all parts of the world; V. Summaries of the contents of the principal archæological periodicals.

The Journal is published quarterly, and forms a yearly volume of about 500 pages royal 8vo, with colored, heliotype and other plates, and numerous figures, at the subscription price of $5.00. Six volumes have been published.

It has been the aim of the editors that the Journal, beside giving a survey of the whole field of Archæology, should be international in character, by affording to the leading archæologists of all countries a common medium for the publication of the results of their labors. This object has been in great part attained, as is shown by the list of eminent foreign and American contributors to the three volumes already issued, and by the character of articles and correspondence published. Not only have important contributions to the advance of the science been made in the original articles, but the present condition of research has been brought before our readers in the departments of Correspondence, and Reviews of the more important recent books. Two departments in which the Journal stands quite alone are (1) the *Record of Discoveries*, and (2) the *Summaries of Periodicals*. In the former a detailed account is given of all discoveries and excavations in every portion of the civilized world, from India to America, especial attention being given to Greece and Italy. In order to insure thoroughness in this work, more than sixty periodical publications are consulted, and material is secured from special correspondents.

In order that readers should know everything of importance that appears in periodical literature, a considerable space has been given to careful summaries of the papers contained in the principal periodicals that treat of Archæology and the Fine Arts. By these various methods, all important work done is concentrated and made accessible in a convenient but scholarly form. equally suited to the specialist and to the general reader.

All literary communications should be addressed to the managing editor,

**A. L. FROTHINGHAM, JR.,**

PRINCETON, N. J.

All business communications to the publishers,

**GINN & COMPANY,**

BOSTON, MASS.

# MODERN LANGUAGE NOTES.

## A MONTHLY PUBLICATION
*With intermission from July to October inclusive.*

### DEVOTED TO THE INTERESTS
#### OF THE
## ACADEMIC STUDY OF ENGLISH, GERMAN
### AND THE
## ROMANCE LANGUAGES.

A. MARSHALL ELLIOTT, *Managing Editor.*
JAMES W. BRIGHT, H. C. G. VON JAGEMANN, HENRY ALFRED TODD,
*Associate Editors.*

This is a successful and widely-known periodical, managed by a corps of professors and instructors in the Johns Hopkins University, with the co-operation of many of the leading college professors, in the department of modern languages, throughout the country. While undertaking to maintain a high critical and scientific standard, the new journal will endeavor to engage the interest and meet the wants of the entire class of serious and progressive modern-language teachers, of whatever grade. Since its establishment in January, 1886, the journal has been repeatedly enlarged, and has met with constantly increasing encouragement and success. The wide range of its articles, original, critical, literary and pedagogical, by a number of the foremost American (and European) scholars, has well represented and recorded the recent progress of modern language studies, both at home and abroad.

The list of contributors to MODERN LANGUAGE NOTES, in addition to the Editors, includes the following names:
ANDERSON, MELVILLE B., State University of Iowa; BANCROFT, T. WHITING, Brown University, R. I.; BASKERVILL, W. M., Vanderbilt University, Tenn.; BOCHER, FERDINAND, Harvard University, Mass.; BRADLEY, C. B., University of California, Cal.; BRANDT, H. C. G., Hamilton College, N. Y.; BROWNE, WM. HAND, Johns Hopkins University, Md.; BURNHAM, WM. H., Johns Hopkins University, Md.; CARPENTER, WM. H., Columbia College, N. Y.; CLÉDAT, L., Faculté des Lettres, Lyons, France; COHN, ADOLPHE, Harvard University, Mass.; COOK, A. S., Yale University; COSIJN, P. J., University of Leyden, Holland; CRANE, T. F., Cornell University, N. Y.; DAVIDSON, THOMAS, Orange, N. J.; EGGE, ALBERT E., St. Olaf's College, Minn.; FAY, E. A., National Deaf-Mute College, Washington, D. C.; FORTIER, ALCÉE, Tulane University, La.; GARNER, SAMUEL, U. S. Naval Academy; GERBER, A., Earlham College, Ind.; GRANDGENT, CHARLES, Harvard University, Mass.; GUMMERE, F. B., The Swain Free School, Mass.; HART, J. M., University of Cincinnati, Ohio; HEMPL, GEO., University of Michigan; HUSS, H. C. O., Princeton College, N. J.; VON JAGEMANN, H. C. G., Harvard University; KARSTEN, GUSTAF, University of Indiana, Ind.; LANG, HENRY R., The Swain Free School, Mass.; LEARNED, M. D., Johns Hopkins University, Md.; LEYH, EDW. F., Baltimore, Md.; LODEMAN, A., State Normal School, Mich.; MORFILL, W. R., Oxford, England; MCCABE, T, Johns Hopkins University, Md.; MCELROY, JOHN G. R., University of Pennsylvania, Pa.; O'CONNOR, B. F., Columbia College, N. Y.; PRIMER, SYLVESTER, Providence, R. I.; SCHELE DE VERE, M., University of Virginia, Va.; SCHILLING, HUGO, Wittenberg College, Ohio; SHELDON, EDW. S., Harvard University, Mass.; SHEPHERD, H. E., College of Charleston, S. C.; SCHMIDT, H., University of Deseret, Salt Lake City, Utah; SIEVERS, EDUARD, University of Tübingen, Germany; SMYTH, A. H., High School of Philadephia, Pa.; STODDARD, FRANCIS H., University of City of New York; STURZINGER, J. J., Bryn Mawr College, Pa.; THOMAS, CALVIN, University of Michigan, Mich.; WALTER, E. L., University of Michigan, Mich.; WARREN, F. M., Johns Hopkins University, Md.; WHITE, H. S., Cornell University, N. Y.

Subscription Price $1.50 per Annum, Payable in Advance.

Foreign Countries $1.75 per Annum.

Single Copies Twenty Cents.    Specimen Pages sent on Application.

Subscriptions, advertisements and all business communications should be addressed to the
MANAGING EDITOR OF MODERN LANGUAGE NOTES,
JOHNS HOPKINS UNIVERSITY, BALTIMORE, MD.

# American Economic Association.

## PUBLICATIONS.

A series of monographs on a great variety of economic subjects, treated in a scientific manner by authors well known in the line of work they here represent.

Among the subjects presented are Coöperation, Socialism, the Laboring Classes, Wages, Capital, Money, Finance, Statistics, Prices, the Relation of the State and Municipality to Private Industry and various Public Works, the Railway Question, Road Legislation, the English Woolen Industry, and numerous other topics of a like nature.

The latest publication is that for January, 1892,—Vol. VII, No. 1,—entitled:

## The Silver Situation in the United States.

### By F. W. Taussig, LL. B., Ph. D.,

*Assistant Professor of Political Economy in Harvard University.*

**118 pages, 8vo.   rice, Seventy-five cents.**

Six volumes of these publications, containing thirty-six numbers, are now complete.

The volumes will be sent, bound in cloth, at $5 each ; any two for $9 ; any three for $13 ; any four for $17 ; any five for $21 ; all six for $25, and including subscription to Vol. VII, $29.   Unbound, $4 per volume.   A few copies bound in half-morocco are offered at $5.50 each ; any two for $10 ; any three for $14.50 ; any four for $19.00 ; any five for $23.50 ; all six for $28.

Annual membership $3 ; life membership $50.

Orders and remittances should be sent to the

PUBLICATION AGENT, AMERICAN ECONOMIC ASSOCIATION, BALTIMORE, MD.

# STUDIES IN HISTORY, ECONOMICS AND PUBLIC LAW,

EDITED BY

## THE UNIVERSITY FACULTY OF POLITICAL SCIENCE OF COLUMBIA COLLEGE.

---

The monographs are chosen mainly from among the doctors' dissertations in Political Science, but are not necessarily confined to these. Only those studies are included which form a distinct contribution to science and which are positive works of original research. The monographs are published at irregular intervals, but are paged consecutively as well as separately, so as to form completed volumes.

The first four numbers in the series are :

1. **The Divorce Problem—A Study in Statistics. By Walter F. Willcox, Ph. D. Price, 50 cents.**

2. **The History of Tariff Administration in the United States, from Colonial Times to the McKinley Administrative Bill. By John Dean Goss, Ph. D. Price, 50 cents.**

3. **History of Municipal Land Ownership on Manhattan Island. By George Ashton Black, Ph. D. Price, 50 cents.**

4. **Financial History of Massachusetts. By Charles H. J. Douglas. Price, $1.00.**

**Volume I. complete. Price, $2.00.**

Other numbers will be announced hereafter.

For further particulars apply to

PROFESSOR EDWIN R. A. SELIGMAN,
COLUMBIA COLLEGE, NEW YORK.

# NOTES SUPPLEMENTARY TO THE STUDIES.

The publication of a series of *Notes* was begun in January, 1889. The following have thus far been issued :

**MUNICIPAL GOVERNMENT IN ENGLAND.** By Dr. ALBERT SHAW, of Minneapolis, Reader on Muuicipal Government, J. H. U.

**SOCIAL WORK IN AUSTRALIA AND LONDON.** By WILLIAM GREY, of the Denison Club, London.

**ENCOURAGEMENT OF HIGHER EDUCATION.** By Professor HERBERT B. ADAMS.

**THE PROBLEM OF CITY GOVERNMENT.** By Hon. SETH LOW, President of Columbia College.

**THE LIBRARIES OF BALTIMORE.** By Mr. P. R. UHLER, of the Peabody Institute.

**WORK AMONG THE WORKINGWOMEN IN BALTIMORE.** By Professor H. B. ADAMS.

**CHARITIES: THE RELATION OF THE STATE, THE CITY, AND THE INDIVIDUAL TO MODERN PHILANTHROPIC WORK.** By A. G. WARNER, Ph. D., sometime General Secretary of the Charity Organization Society of Baltimore, now Associate Professor in the University of Nebraska.

**LAW AND HISTORY.** By WALTER B. SCAIFE, LL. B., Ph. D. (Vienna), Reader on Historical Geography in the Johns Hopkins University.

**THE NEEDS OF SELF-SUPPORTING WOMEN.** By Miss CLARE DE GRAFFENREID, of the Department of Labor, Washington, D. C.

**THE ENOCH PRATT FREE LIBRARY.** By LEWIS H. STEINER, Litt. D.

**EARLY PRESBYTERIANISM IN MARYLAND.** By Rev. J. W. MCILVAIN.

**THE EDUCATIONAL ASPECT OF THE U. S. NATIONAL MUSEUM.** By Professor O. T. MASON.

**UNIVERSITY EXTENSION AND THE UNIVERSITY OF THE FUTURE.** By RICHARD G. MOULTON.

*These Notes are sent without charge to regular subscribers to the Studies. They are sold at five cents each; twenty-five copies will be furnished for $1.00.*

## ANNUAL SERIES, 1883-1891.

Nine Series of the University Studies are now complete and will be sold, bound in cloth, as follows:

**SERIES I.—LOCAL INSTITUTIONS.** 479 pp. $4.00.
**SERIES II.—INSTITUTIONS AND ECONOMICS.** 629 pp. $4.00.
**SERIES III.—MARYLAND, VIRGINIA, AND WASHINGTON.** 595 pp. $4.00.
**SERIES IV.—MUNICIPAL GOVERNMENT AND LAND TENURE.** 600 pp. $3.50.
**SERIES V.—MUNICIPAL GOVERNMENT, HISTORY AND POLITICS.** 559 pp. $3.50.
**SERIES VI.—THE HISTORY OF CO-OPERATION IN THE UNITED STATES.** 540 pp. $3.50.
**SERIES VII.—SOCIAL SCIENCE, MUNICIPAL AND FEDERAL GOVERNMENT.** 628 pp. $3.50.
**SERIES VIII.—HISTORY, POLITICS, AND EDUCATION.** 625 pp. $3.50.
**SERIES IX.—EDUCATION, POLITICS AND SOCIAL SCIENCE.** 640 pp. $3.50.

*The set of nine volumes is now offered, uniformly bound in cloth, for library use, for $27.00. The nine volumes, with nine extra volumes, "New Haven," "Baltimore," "Philadelphia," "Local Constitutional History," Vol. I, "Negro in Maryland," "U. S. Supreme Court," "U. S. and Japan," "Switzerland," and "Spanish Institutions in the Southwest," altogether eighteen volumes in cloth, for $40.00. The seven extra volumes (now ready) will be furnished together for $13.50.*

All business communications should be addressed to THE JOHNS HOPKINS PRESS, BALTIMORE, MARYLAND. Subscriptions will also be received, or single copies furnished by any of the following

### AMERICAN AGENTS :

**New York.**—G. P. Putnam's Sons.
**New Haven.**—E. P. Judd.
**Boston.**—Damrell & Upham; W. B. Clarke & Co.
**Providence.**—Tibbitts & Preston.
**Philadelphia.**—Porter & Coates; J. B. Lippincott Co.
**Washington.**—W. H. Lowdermilk & Co.; Brentano's.

**Cincinnati.**—Robert Clarke & Co.
**Indianapolis.**—Bowen-Merrill Co.
**Chicago.**—A. C. McClurg & Co.
**Louisville.**—Flexner Brothers.
**San Francisco.**—Bancroft Company.
**New Orleans.**—George F. Wharton.
**Richmond.**—J. W. Randolph & Co.
**Toronto.**—Carswell Co. (Limited).
**Montreal.**—William Foster Brown & Co.

### EUROPEAN AGENTS :

**Paris.**—A. Hermann; Em. Terquem.
**Strassburg.**—Karl J. Trübner.
**Berlin.**—Puttkammer & Mühlbrecht; Mayer & Müller.
**Leipzig.**—F. A. Brockhaus.

**London.**—Kegan Paul, Trench, Trübner & Co.; G. P. Putnam's Sons.
**Frankfort.**—Joseph Baer & Co.
**Turin, Florence, and Rome.**—E. Loescher.

# THE REPUBLIC OF NEW HAVEN.

## A HISTORY OF MUNICIPAL EVOLUTION.

### By CHARLES H. LEVERMORE, Ph. D.

*(Extra Volume One of Studies in Historical and Political Science.)*

The volume comprises 342 pages octavo, with various diagrams and an index. It will be sold, bound in cloth, at $2.00.

---

# PHILADELPHIA, 1681-1887:

## A HISTORY OF MUNICIPAL DEVELOPMENT.

### By EDWARD P. ALLINSON, A. M., AND BOIES PENROSE, A. B.

*(Extra Volume Two of Studies in Historical and Political Science.)*

The volume comprises 444 pages octavo, and will be sold, bound in cloth, at $3.00; in law-sheep at $3.50.

---

# Baltimore and the Nineteenth of April, 1861.

## A STUDY OF THE WAR.

### By GEORGE WILLIAM BROWN,

*Chief Judge of the Supreme Bench of Baltimore, and Mayor of the City in 1861.*

*(Extra Volume Three of Studies in Historical and Political Science.)*

The volume comprises 176 pages octavo, and will be sold, bound in cloth, at $1.

---

# Local Constitutional History of the United States.

### By GEORGE E. HOWARD,

*Professor of History in the University of Nebraska.*

*(Extra Volumes Four and Five of Studies in Historical and Political Science.)*

Volume I.—Development of the Township, Hundred and Shire. Now ready. 542 pp. 8vo. Cloth. Price, $3.00.

Volume II.—Development of the City and Local Magistracies. In preparation.

---

# THE NEGRO IN MARYLAND.

## A STUDY OF THE INSTITUTION OF SLAVERY.

### By JEFFREY R. BRACKETT, Ph. D.

*(Extra Volume Six of Studies in Historical and Political Science.)*

270 pages octavo, in cloth. $2.00.

---

The extra volumes are sold at reduced rates to regular subscribers to the "Studies."

# The Supreme Court of the United States.

## Its History and Influence in our Constitutional System.

### By W. W. WILLOUGHBY, PH. D.

Extra Vol. VII of the Studies in History and Politics.

**124 pages. 8vo. Cloth. Price, $1.25.**

---

# The Intercourse between the U.S. and Japan.

### By INAZO (OTA) NITOBE, PH. D.,
#### Associate Professor, Sapporo, Japan.

Extra Vol. VIII of the Studies in History and Politics.

**198 pages. 8vo. Cloth. Price, $1.25.**

---

# State and Federal Government in Switzerland.

### By JOHN MARTIN VINCENT, PH. D.,
#### Librarian and Instructor in the Department of History and Politics, Johns Hopkins University.

Extra Vol. IX of the Studies in History and Politics.

**225 pages. 8vo. Cloth. Price, $1.50.**

In view of the fact that the six-hundredth anniversary of the foundation of Federal Government in Switzerland is celebrated in 1891, this may be considered a timely book. The history and constitutional experiments of Switzerland have, however, a perennial interest for Americans, for in no other country do governmental institutions approach more closely, in form and principle, those found in the United States. The present work is essentially a study of modern institutions, but always with reference to their source and development.

---

# Spanish Institutions of the Southwest.

### By FRANK W. BLACKMAR, Ph. D.
#### Professor of History and Sociology in the Kansas State University.

Extra Vol. X of the Studies in History and Politics.

**380 pages. 8vo. Cloth. Price, $2.00.**

With Thirty-one Historical Illustrations of old Spanish Missions, etc., and a map showing the extent of Spanish Possessions in North America in 1783.

This work is a study of the Social and Political Institutions of Spain, as represented by the life of the Spanish colonists in America. A sufficient amount of descriptive history is given to relieve the subject from the monotony of abstract discussion and to subtantiate all conclusions reached by the writer. The book treats of the founding of the Spanish missions in California, Arizona, New Mexico, and Texas, and portrays the civilization established by the *padres*, the social condition of the Indians, and the political and social life of the pioneers of the Southwest. It represents the government, laws, municipal organization, and life of the colonists. The movement of the civil, religious, and military powers in the "temporal and spiritual conquest," and the consequent founding of civic pueblos, missions and military towns are fully discussed.

There are thirty-one illustrations, chiefly historical. They reveal some of the most picturesque ruins of America.

Orders should be addressed to THE JOHNS HOPKINS PRESS, BALTIMORE, MARYLAND.